MW00885390

a Queen is not afraid to Fail

NOBODY GIVES YOU POWER

MEALS / FOOD

MISCELLANEOUS

REUNIONS/FRIENDS	IMPORTANT STUFF	NOTES/REMINDERS	APPOINTMENTS	EXERCISE ROUTINE	FUN STUFF, SHOPPING, ETC
					M
					T
					W
					T
					F
					S
					S

MONDAY

TUESDAY

WEDNESDAY

THURSDAY

FRIDAY

SATURDAY-SUNDAY

I will speak with confidence and self assurance.

Every day brings new opportunities.

MEALS / FOOD

MISCELLANEOUS

REUNIONS/FRIENDS	IMPORTANT STUFF	NOTES/REMINDERS	APPOINTMENTS	EXERCISE ROUTINE	FUN STUFF, SHOPPING, ETC
					M
					T
					W
					T
					F
					S
					S

MONDAY

TUESDAY

WEDNESDAY

THURSDAY

FRIDAY

SATURDAY-SUNDAY

I have faith in myself.

Whatever I do, I give my best.

MEALS / FOOD

MISCELLANEOUS

REUNIONS/FRIENDS	IMPORTANT STUFF	NOTES/REMINDERS	APPOINTMENTS	EXERCISE ROUTINE	FUN STUFF, SHOPPING, ETC
					M
					T
					W
					T
					F
					S
					S

MONDAY

TUESDAY

WEDNESDAY

THURSDAY

FRIDAY

SATURDAY-SUNDAY

I am loved and I am wanted.

I have a beautiful imagination.

MEALS / FOOD

MISCELLANEOUS

REUNIONS/FRIENDS	IMPORTANT STUFF	NOTES/REMINDERS	APPOINTMENTS	EXERCISE ROUTINE	FUN STUFF, SHOPPING, ETC.
					M
					T
					W
					T
					F
					S
					S

MONDAY

TUESDAY

WEDNESDAY

THURSDAY

FRIDAY

SATURDAY-SUNDAY

I have good friends.

I get better and better every day.

MEALS / FOOD

MISCELLANEOUS

REUNIONS/FRIENDS	IMPORTANT STUFF	NOTES/REMINDERS	APPOINTMENTS	EXERCISE ROUTINE	FUN STUFF, SHOPPING, ETC
					M
					T
					W
					T
					F
					S
					S

MONDAY

TUESDAY

WEDNESDAY

THURSDAY

FRIDAY

SATURDAY-SUNDAY

I am grateful for the things I have.

I will achieve all of my goals.

MEALS / FOOD

MISCELLANEOUS

REUNIONS/FRIENDS	IMPORTANT STUFF	NOTES/REMINDERS	APPOINTMENTS	EXERCISE ROUTINE	FUN STUFF, SHOPPING, ETC
					M
					T
					W
					T
					F
					S
					S

MONDAY

TUESDAY

WEDNESDAY

THURSDAY

FRIDAY

SATURDAY-SUNDAY

I will accept nothing but the best.

I am constantly improving.

MEALS / FOOD

MISCELLANEOUS

REUNIONS/FRIENDS	IMPORTANT STUFF	NOTES/REMINDERS	APPOINTMENTS	EXERCISE ROUTINE	FUN STUFF, SHOPPING, ETC
					M
					T
					W
					T
					F
					S
					S

MONDAY

TUESDAY

WEDNESDAY

THURSDAY

FRIDAY

SATURDAY-SUNDAY

I desire to learn new things.

The little things in life make all the difference.

MEALS / FOOD

MISCELLANEOUS

REUNIONS/FRIENDS

IMPORTANT STUFF

NOTES/REMINDERS

APPOINTMENTS

EXERCISE ROUTINE

FUN STUFF, SHOPPING, ETC

					M
					T
					W
					T
					F
					S
					S

MONDAY

TUESDAY

WEDNESDAY

THURSDAY

FRIDAY

SATURDAY-SUNDAY

My thoughts are positive and full of joy.

I am unique and a gift to the world.

MEALS / FOOD

MISCELLANEOUS

REUNIONS/FRIENDS	IMPORTANT STUFF	NOTES/REMINDERS	APPOINTMENTS	EXERCISE ROUTINE	FUN STUFF, SHOPPING, ETC
					M
					T
					W
					T
					F
					S
					S

MONDAY

TUESDAY

WEDNESDAY

THURSDAY

FRIDAY

SATURDAY-SUNDAY

I am calm and confident.

I am open to new and exciting possibilities.

MEALS / FOOD

MISCELLANEOUS

REUNIONS/FRIENDS	IMPORTANT STUFF	NOTES/REMINDERS	APPOINTMENTS	EXERCISE ROUTINE	FUN STUFF, SHOPPING, ETC
					M
					T
					W
					T
					F
					S
					S

MONDAY

TUESDAY

WEDNESDAY

THURSDAY

FRIDAY

SATURDAY-SUNDAY

I am strong, inside and out.

Miracles happen to me.

MEALS / FOOD

MISCELLANEOUS

REUNIONS/FRIENDS	IMPORTANT STUFF	NOTES/REMINDERS	APPOINTMENTS	EXERCISE ROUTINE	FUN STUFF, SHOPPING, ETC
					M
					T
					W
					T
					F
					S
					S

MONDAY

TUESDAY

WEDNESDAY

THURSDAY

FRIDAY

SATURDAY-SUNDAY

I am patient.

I am perfect just the way I am.

MEALS / FOOD

MISCELLANEOUS

REUNIONS/FRIENDS	IMPORTANT STUFF	NOTES/REMINDERS	APPOINTMENTS	EXERCISE ROUTINE	FUN STUFF, SHOPPING, ETC
					M
					T
					W
					T
					F
					S
					S

MONDAY

TUESDAY

WEDNESDAY

THURSDAY

FRIDAY

SATURDAY-SUNDAY

I keep my body healthy.

I am important.

MEALS / FOOD

MISCELLANEOUS

REUNIONS/FRIENDS	IMPORTANT STUFF	NOTES/REMINDERS	APPOINTMENTS	EXERCISE ROUTINE	FUN STUFF, SHOPPING, ETC.	
						M
						T
						W
						T
						F
						S
						S

MONDAY

TUESDAY

WEDNESDAY

THURSDAY

FRIDAY

SATURDAY-SUNDAY

I can do anything.

I approve of myself.

MEALS / FOOD

MISCELLANEOUS

REUNIONS/FRIENDS	IMPORTANT STUFF	NOTES/REMINDERS	APPOINTMENTS	EXERCISE ROUTINE	FUN STUFF, SHOPPING, ETC.
					M
					T
					W
					T
					F
					S
					S

MONDAY

TUESDAY

WEDNESDAY

THURSDAY

FRIDAY

SATURDAY-SUNDAY

I trust my intuition.

My heart guides me.

MEALS / FOOD

MISCELLANEOUS

REUNIONS/FRIENDS	IMPORTANT STUFF	NOTES/REMINDERS	APPOINTMENTS	EXERCISE ROUTINE	FUN STUFF, SHOPPING, ETC.
					M
					T
					W
					T
					F
					S
					S

MONDAY

TUESDAY

WEDNESDAY

THURSDAY

FRIDAY

SATURDAY-SUNDAY

I am thankful for being who I am.

FAITH. FAMILY. FORGIVENESS.

MEALS / FOOD

MISCELLANEOUS

REUNIONS/FRIENDS	IMPORTANT STUFF	NOTES/REMINDERS	APPOINTMENTS	EXERCISE ROUTINE	FUN STUFF, SHOPPING, ETC
					M
					T
					W
					T
					F
					S
					S

MONDAY

TUESDAY

WEDNESDAY

THURSDAY

FRIDAY

SATURDAY-SUNDAY

I support others with love and kindness.

I am a winner.

MEALS / FOOD

MISCELLANEOUS

REUNIONS/FRIENDS	IMPORTANT STUFF	NOTES/REMINDERS	APPOINTMENTS	EXERCISE ROUTINE	FUN STUFF, SHOPPING, ETC
					M
					T
					W
					T
					F
					S
					S

MONDAY

TUESDAY

WEDNESDAY

THURSDAY

FRIDAY

SATURDAY-SUNDAY

GLOW. GRATITUDE. GROW.

I am beautiful.

MEALS / FOOD

MISCELLANEOUS

REUNIONS/FRIENDS	IMPORTANT STUFF	NOTES/REMINDERS	APPOINTMENTS	EXERCISE ROUTINE	FUN STUFF, SHOPPING, ETC
					M
					T
					W
					T
					F
					S
					S

MONDAY

TUESDAY

WEDNESDAY

THURSDAY

FRIDAY

SATURDAY-SUNDAY

I am excited of the unknown.

HOPE. HARMONY. HUMBLE.

MEALS / FOOD

MISCELLANEOUS

REUNIONS/FRIENDS	IMPORTANT STUFF	NOTES/REMINDERS	APPOINTMENTS	EXERCISE ROUTINE	FUN STUFF, SHOPPING, ETC
					M
					T
					W
					T
					F
					S
					S

MONDAY

TUESDAY

WEDNESDAY

THURSDAY

FRIDAY

SATURDAY-SUNDAY

I receive all the help that I need.

Everything works out just fine.

MEALS / FOOD

MISCELLANEOUS

REUNIONS/FRIENDS	IMPORTANT STUFF	NOTES/REMINDERS	APPOINTMENTS	EXERCISE ROUTINE	FUN STUFF, SHOPPING, ETC
					M
					T
					W
					T
					F
					S
					S

MONDAY

TUESDAY

WEDNESDAY

THURSDAY

FRIDAY

SATURDAY-SUNDAY

Wonderful and awesome things happen to me.

IMAGINATION. INSPIRE. INTEGRITY.

MEALS / FOOD

MISCELLANEOUS

REUNIONS/FRIENDS	IMPORTANT STUFF	NOTES/REMINDERS	APPOINTMENTS	EXERCISE ROUTINE	FUN STUFF, SHOPPING, ETC
					M
					T
					W
					T
					F
					S
					S

MONDAY

TUESDAY

WEDNESDAY

THURSDAY

FRIDAY

SATURDAY-SUNDAY

I forgive myself for making a mistake.

LOVE. LOYAL. LIFE.

MEALS / FOOD

MISCELLANEOUS

REUNIONS/FRIENDS	IMPORTANT STUFF	NOTES/REMINDERS	APPOINTMENTS	EXERCISE ROUTINE	FUN STUFF, SHOPPING, ETC
					M
					T
					W
					T
					F
					S
					S

MONDAY

TUESDAY

WEDNESDAY

THURSDAY

FRIDAY

SATURDAY-SUNDAY

I believe in myself.

I believe in my dreams.

MEALS / FOOD

MISCELLANEOUS

REUNIONS/FRIENDS	IMPORTANT STUFF	NOTES/REMINDERS	APPOINTMENTS	EXERCISE ROUTINE	FUN STUFF, SHOPPING, ETC
					M
					T
					W
					T
					F
					S
					S

MONDAY

TUESDAY

WEDNESDAY

THURSDAY

FRIDAY

SATURDAY-SUNDAY

I have the courage to be myself.

MIRACLE. MINDFUL. MELLOW.

MEALS / FOOD

MISCELLANEOUS

REUNIONS/FRIENDS	IMPORTANT STUFF	NOTES/REMINDERS	APPOINTMENTS	EXERCISE ROUTINE	FUN STUFF, SHOPPING, ETC
					M
					T
					W
					T
					F
					S
					S

MONDAY

TUESDAY

WEDNESDAY

THURSDAY

FRIDAY

SATURDAY-SUNDAY

I am okay with who I am.

What makes you smile?

MEALS / FOOD

MISCELLANEOUS

REUNIONS/FRIENDS	IMPORTANT STUFF	NOTES/REMINDERS	APPOINTMENTS	EXERCISE ROUTINE	FUN STUFF, SHOPPING, ETC
					M
					T
					W
					T
					F
					S
					S

MONDAY

TUESDAY

WEDNESDAY

THURSDAY

FRIDAY

SATURDAY-SUNDAY

Write about a place you would like to visit someday?

How can you give back to your community?

MEALS / FOOD

MISCELLANEOUS

REUNIONS/FRIENDS	IMPORTANT STUFF	NOTES/REMINDERS	APPOINTMENTS	EXERCISE ROUTINE	FUN STUFF, SHOPPING, ETC
					M
					T
					W
					T
					F
					S
					S

MONDAY

TUESDAY

WEDNESDAY

THURSDAY

FRIDAY

SATURDAY-SUNDAY

What is the best gift you ever received?

Write about four things that your family has taught you.

MEALS / FOOD

MISCELLANEOUS

REUNIONS/FRIENDS	IMPORTANT STUFF	NOTES/REMINDERS	APPOINTMENTS	EXERCISE ROUTINE	FUN STUFF, SHOPPING, ETC
					M
					T
					W
					T
					F
					S
					S

MONDAY

TUESDAY

WEDNESDAY

THURSDAY

FRIDAY

SATURDAY-SUNDAY

Name 5 things you like about yourself and why.

MEALS / FOOD

MISCELLANEOUS

REUNIONS/FRIENDS	IMPORTANT STUFF	NOTES/REMINDERS	APPOINTMENTS	EXERCISE ROUTINE	FUN STUFF, SHOPPING, ETC
					M
					T
					W
					T
					F
					S
					S

MONDAY

TUESDAY

WEDNESDAY

THURSDAY

FRIDAY

SATURDAY-SUNDAY

55606076R00064

Made in the USA
San Bernardino,
CA